EVOLVE

WORKBOOK

Carolyn Clarke Flores and Michele Lewis

5A

Shaftesbury Road, Cambridge CB2 8EA, United Kingdom

One Liberty Plaza, 20th Floor, New York, NY 10006, USA

477 Williamstown Road, Port Melbourne, VIC 3207, Australia

314–321, 3rd Floor, Plot 3, Splendor Forum, Jasola District Centre, New Delhi – 110025, India

103 Penang Road, #05-06/07, Visioncrest Commercial, Singapore 238467

Cambridge University Press & Assessment is a department of the University of Cambridge.

We share the University's mission to contribute to society through the pursuit of education, learning and research at the highest international levels of excellence.

www.cambridge.org
Information on this title: www.cambridge.org/9781108408813

First published 2020

20 19 18 17 16 15 14 13 12 11 10 9 8 7 6

Printed and bound by CPI Group (UK) Ltd, Croydon, CR0 4YY

A catalogue record for this publication is available from the British Library

ISBN 978-1-108-40533-1 Student's Book
ISBN 978-1-108-40511-9 Student's Book A
ISBN 978-1-108-40926-1 Student's Book B
ISBN 978-1-108-40534-8 Student's Book with Practice Extra
ISBN 978-1-108-40513-3 Student's Book with Practice Extra A
ISBN 978-1-108-40927-8 Student's Book with Practice Extra B
ISBN 978-1-108-40907-0 Workbook with Audio
ISBN 978-1-108-40881-3 Workbook with Audio A
ISBN 978-1-108-41195-0 Workbook with Audio B
ISBN 978-1-108-40519-5 Teacher's Edition with Test Generator
ISBN 978-1-108-41074-8 Presentation Plus
ISBN 978-1-108-41205-6 Class Audio CDs
ISBN 978-1-108-40800-4 Video Resource Book with DVD
ISBN 978-1-108-41450-0 Full Contact with DVD
ISBN 978-1-108-41156-1 Full Contact with DVD A
ISBN 978-1-108-41421-0 Full Contact with DVD B

Additional resources for this publication at www.cambridge.org/evolve

CONTENTS

UNIT 1 STEP FORWARD

1.1 LIFE CHANGES

1 VOCABULARY: Facing challenges

A **Complete the sentences with the words in the box.**

accept	adapt	resist	survive	tackle	~~underestimate~~	welcome

1 Law school students often *underestimate* the amount of homework they will get. It is usually more than they expected.

2 Marisol finally decided to ______ graduate school. She plans to start next year.

3 She didn't take the job because she couldn't ______ the low salary.

4 When Daniel moved from Boston to Phoenix, it took him a few months to ______ to the hot climate.

5 I did not think I would ______ my first year as a doctor because it was so difficult. Luckily, kind coworkers helped me get through it.

6 If you ______ making changes in your life, you won't grow or have new experiences.

7 My boss told me I was ______ to participate in the meeting.

B **Match the challenges with the correct solution.**

1 You can't take crowds. *e*

2 You're capable of managing people. ___

3 You underestimated the amount of time you needed. ___

4 You're frightened of getting lost. ___

5 You got through medical school. ___

6 You want to take a step forward in your career. ___

7 You can't get a grip on Spanish. ___

8 You can't cope with studying for a higher degree. ___

a Study in Mexico.

b Use a good map.

c Don't go to graduate school.

d Look for training opportunities.

e Don't move to a big city.

f You expect to earn a good salary.

g You'll be a good boss.

h Schedule more time for the task.

2 GRAMMAR: Present habits

A **Circle the correct answer to complete each sentence.**

1 Ivan ___ friends easily. He'll meet a lot of new people when he moves.

- **a** tends to making
- **(b)** tends to make
- **c** is making

2 When I'm looking for a new job, ___ to as many companies as possible.

- **a** I'm applying
- **b** I applied
- **c** I apply

3 I ____ trying to learn new skills. I think that's the key to success.

a am constantly

b tend to

c constantly

4 When I take a difficult class, I ____ my professor for help at least once a week.

a am asking

b always asking

c ask

5 I ____ for different ways to stay healthy. Yesterday, I went to a new exercise class.

a always look

b always looking

c am always look

6 When ____ bored with my classes, I think about changing my major.

a feel

b I'm feeling

c I'm feel

B **Complete the sentences using the correct form of the verbs in parentheses.**

1 I'm always ____wondering____ what my life will be like when I ____retire____. (wonder, retire)

2 When she's ____________ stressed, she usually ____________ her friend Stephan for support. (feel, call)

3 He tends to ____________ more after he ____________ a new exercise routine. (eat, start)

4 I often ____________ about changing my career to something completely different. (think)

5 He's always ____________ his friends that they should travel if they ever ____________ the chance. (tell, get)

6 I tend to ____________ very excited for people when they ____________ they're getting married. (get, announce)

7 He's always ____________ for new opportunities to make money and will ____________ all of his friends to support him. (look, ask)

3 GRAMMAR AND VOCABULARY

A **Complete the sentences so that they are true for you.**

1 I tend to resist ____trying new kinds of food____.

2 I usually underestimate ____________.

3 I'm feeling encouraged by ____________.

4 I survive difficult times by ____________.

5 I'm always adapting to ____________.

6 I tend to accept ____________.

B **Write three more sentences with information that is true for you. Use *tend to*, *will*, and the present continuous.**

____

____

____

____

____

1.2 MEMORY LANE

1 VOCABULARY: Describing annoying things

A **Choose the correct words or phrases to complete each sentence.**

1 I always feel ______ when I give a presentation. I don't like to speak in public.
   (a) awkward   b frustrating
2 I study Arabic and I think the grammar is ______ . I don't fully understand it yet.
   a a waste of time   b complex
3 It takes time to find a new job, so don't ______ . Just take a break, and then try again.
   a lose patience   b get on your nerves
4 Can you please stop whistling? It's starting to ______ .
   a drive you crazy   b get on my nerves
5 To me, nothing is more ______ than when coworkers are late for a meeting.
   a time-consuming   b infuriating
6 I used to think school was ______ . When I got older, I realized how valuable it had been.
   a a waste of time   b clumsy
7 The early days of the internet were ______ because it took a long time to connect to websites, and then the connection was frequently lost.
   a frustrating   b hard to operate
8 Writing a research paper is so ______ . I wish I could write more quickly.
   a tricky   b time-consuming
9 I remember my first cell phone. It was ______ until I learned how it worked. Then, it was very easy.
   a time-consuming   b hard to operate
10 Understanding modern technology can be ______ , especially for people from older generations who didn't grow up with it.
   a tricky   b hard to operate

2 GRAMMAR: Past habits

A **Correct the mistakes in each sentence. There may be more than one way to correct each mistake.**

1 When I got sick, my grandmother would ~~made~~ make me chicken soup.
2 Before texting, we don't use to be in touch with our friends so often.
3 I would ate soup every day until I felt better.
4 I used to love go to the video store to rent movies.
5 My parents didn't used to let me watch a lot of television.
6 We used to played cards and board games instead.
7 I never use to like playing video games.
8 I am used to read books on rainy days.

B **Change the sentences to show past habits. Use *(not/never) used to* or *would (not)*. There may be more than one answer.**

1 They exchanged gifts on the holidays.

They would exchange gifts on the holidays.

2 She cuts her daughter's hair.

3 He took a lot of photographs.

4 We don't play video games.

5 I picked them up from school.

6 You never study for your exams.

3 GRAMMAR AND VOCABULARY

A **Imagine you grew up in a time without the inventions in the box below. Write sentences about your past habits before these inventions. Use (*not/never*) *used to*, or *would* (*not*) and the vocabulary from exercise 1A.**

cars electricity eye glasses internet ~~smartphones~~ washing machines

1 It used to be frustrating to travel to new cities before smartphones were invented because I would often get lost.

2

3

4

5

6

1.3 UPGRADE

1 LISTENING

A 🔊 1.01 **Listen to the conversation and circle the correct answer.**

1 According to Professor Silva, what is confusing for the students?
  - **a** how they survived without smartphones in the past
  - **b** the different rules on smartphones in class
  - **c** why they have to have discussions with each other in class

2 What does Professor Novak think about smartphones in class?
  - **a** She uses them too much.
  - **b** They're useful in a lot of ways.
  - **c** They shouldn't be allowed.

3 By the end of the conversation, both professors:
  - **a** lose their patience.
  - **b** disagree with each other.
  - **c** agree that cell phones can help students.

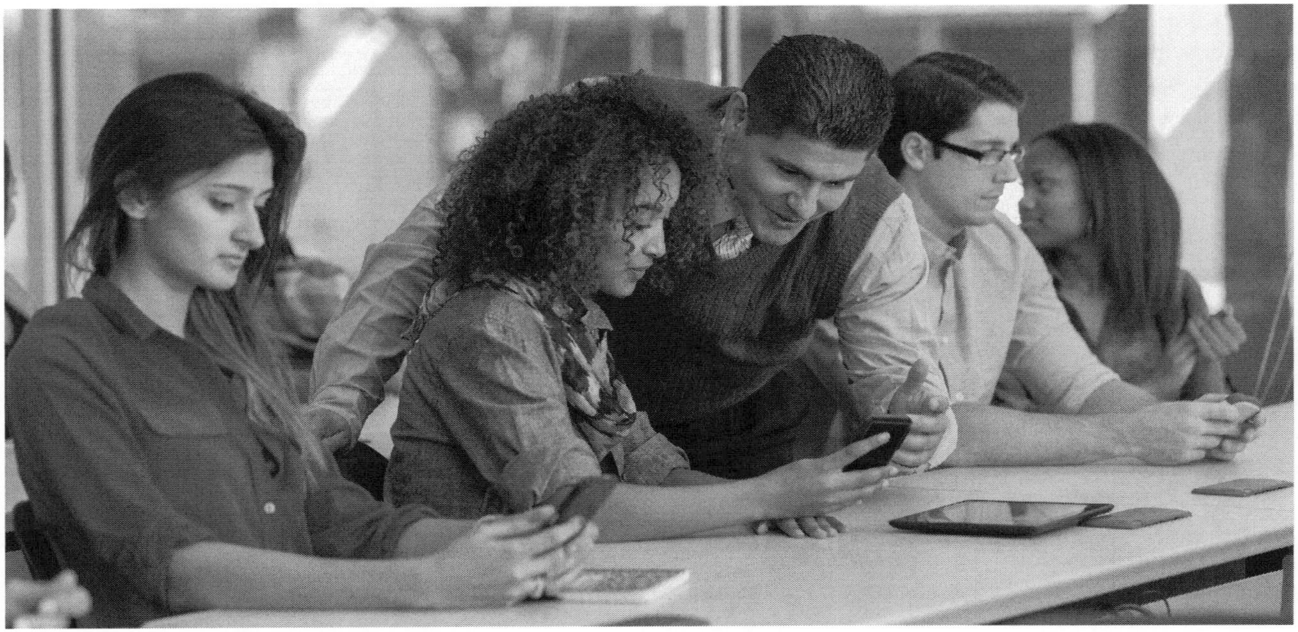

2 CRITICAL THINKING

A THINK CRITICALLY **What are the advantages and disadvantages of using a smartphone in a language class? How could it help you with reading, pronunciation, and listening?**

3 SPEAKING

A **Put the conversation in order.**

___ **A** Yeah, standing in line for tickets and popcorn was part of the excitement. Generally speaking, movies aren't as much fun now. Sure, you can watch from home, but you have to watch it alone or with only a few friends. It was better watching a great movie with a big crowd of people.

___ **B** Count me in! As for *Star Wars*, I have a costume for almost every character. I'll be there.

1 **A** It's so easy to watch movies nowadays, but I really miss going to the theater.

___ **A** When it comes to wearing costumes, I usually have a costume party every time a new *Star Wars* movie comes out. You should come next time. It'll be a lot of fun.

___ **B** That is so true! Remember when the first *Harry Potter* movie came out? There were so many people there. Everyone wore costumes of their favorite characters. It was like a big party.

___ **B** I couldn't agree more. I miss it, too. Overall, watching movies is easy nowadays, but it's also boring. I used to love standing in line to get tickets, buy popcorn …

B **Choose one of the topics. Write a conversation between two people. Use phrases for discussing issues and agreeing strongly.**

1 People are healthier now than they used to be.
2 We used to communicate with each other more frequently.
3 Classroom teaching has improved because of technology.
4 Social media is a waste of time.

A ______________________________

____

B ______________________________

____

A ______________________________

____

B ______________________________

____

A ______________________________

____

B ______________________________

____

1.4 BACK TO BASICS

1 READING

A IDENTIFY MAIN IDEAS **What types of activities could tourists do on a farm? Make a list and then read the text to check your answers.**

TAKING TOURISM
BACK TO ITS ROOTS

Home News About

These days, it often seems like computers do everything for us. But even with all the progress that technology has made, there is comfort in the traditional ways of life. That's why agritourism is on the rise and should continue to be promoted.

Agritourism refers to activities for tourists that take place on a farm or a ranch. There are two main goals of agritourism: to provide meaningful experiences for tourists and to help the farm industry stay alive. The farming economy has suffered. The cost of farm equipment has increased and younger generations don't want to cope with the difficult life of farming, so there is no one to carry on the work.

However, agritourism, which is a branch of eco-tourism, is now a fast-growing part of the travel and tourism economy, and is helping the farm industry improve.

Perhaps you've taken part in this style of tourism without knowing it. Many experiences count as agritourism, such as touring a ranch or visiting a vineyard. Maybe you've visited a farm and collected fresh eggs, or learned to perform some of the many farming tasks that must be tackled on a daily basis.

Because there is agritourism around the world, many opportunities are available. Tourists can spend the weekend at a farm in the California mountains where they learn how to milk a cow and make cheese, but they can also take tea plantation tours in Taiwan, gather figs at a fig farm in Spain, and enjoy many other experiences where they can be close to nature.

Overall, ranches and farms welcome agritourism. One American study found that in the state of Virginia alone, agritourism supported more than 20,000 jobs and generated $840 million in income. It has been a big step forward in keeping the farming industry alive.

B IDENTIFY SPECIFIC INFORMATION **Read the article again. Then answer the questions.**

1 How do tourists benefit from agritourism? ______

2 How does the farm industry benefit from agritourism? ______

3 Why has the farming economy suffered in recent years? ______

4 What states and countries are mentioned where tourists can experience agritourism? ______

5 How did agritourism benefit the state of Virginia? ______

C IDENTIFY SPECIFIC INFORMATION **Read the article again. Find three agritourism activities a tourist may experience.**

______

2 CRITICAL THINKING

A THINK CRITICALLY **Why do you think the agritourism industry has become so successful? Would you be interested in an agritourism experience? Why or why not?**

______

3 WRITING

A **The extracts are from an opinion essay about tourism. They are the beginning of each of the four paragraphs. Decide which paragraph each extract belongs in: first, second, third, or fourth.**

1 Another problem is the impact of tourists on the environment. For example, one beach in Thailand is so popular that tourists create more garbage than the island can cope with. As a result, a lot of plastic, cans, and other damaging items end up in the ocean.

Paragraph: ____________

2 Tourists around the world tend to visit the same places again and again. Everyone wants to see Times Square in New York City or the Grand Palace in Bangkok. However, I think visiting these popular destinations should be discouraged. Too many tourists in one place causes a lot of problems.

Paragraph: ____________

3 Of course, it's understandable that tourists want to see popular places because they are interesting. However, it's time to think more about the problems that welcoming too many tourists can cause.

Paragraph: ____________

4 The first reason tourists should consider non-popular destinations is because of overcrowding.

Paragraph: ____________

B **Complete the chart below with the advantages and disadvantages of tourism in a popular destination. Then write a paragraph about whether you agree or disagree that too much tourism can have a negative effect. Use *the first* and *the second*, or *first*, *next*, and *then* to organize your ideas.**

Advantages	Disadvantages

CHECK AND REVIEW

Read the statements. Can you do these things?

UNIT 1

Mark the boxes. ✔ I can do it. ? I am not sure.	**I can …**	If you are not sure, go back to these pages in the Student's Book.
VOCABULARY	☐ **describe dealing with change.** ☐ **describing annoying things.**	page 2 page 4
GRAMMAR	☐ **use the simple present and the present continuous to describe past habits.** ☐ **express annoyance.**	page 3 page 5
LISTENING AND SPEAKING SKILLS	☐ **listen for opinions.** ☐ **use expressions for discussing views on issues.**	page 6 page 7
READING AND WRITING SKILLS	☐ **identify main ideas and specific information.** ☐ **organize information in an opinion essay.**	page 8 page 9

UNIT 2 NATURAL LIMITS

2.1 DEEP OCEAN OR DEEP SPACE?

1 VOCABULARY: Space and ocean exploration

A **Circle the correct word to complete the sentences.**

1 Some companies think they will be able to *launch* / *monitor* tourists into space within the next few years.
2 The researchers want to *use up* / *preserve* the natural beauty of the ocean.
3 Some experts are worried that humans will *use up* / *come across* the Earth's supply of oil one day.
4 I bought a telescope so I can *preserve* / *observe* the stars at night.
5 The equipment used to *monitor* / *come across* the ocean floor is very expensive.
6 Underwater vehicles are often used for ocean *exploration* / *atmosphere*.
7 Sometimes, *resources* / *satellites* are used to predict the weather.
8 Scientists are continuing their *resources* / *investigation* into why the rocket exploded upon take-off.
9 Too much pollution can create a dirty and unpleasant *atmosphere* / *species*.
10 The ocean contains many useful *resources* / *investigations*, such as salt, sand, copper, and oil.
11 Many *species* / *satellites* that live in the ocean are still being studied by scientists.
12 The tourists didn't *launched* / *come across* any rare type of fish on their boat trip.
13 I love to float on the *atmosphere* / *surface* of the water. It's so relaxing.

2 GRAMMAR: Comparative structures

A **Circle the correct word to complete each sentence.**

1 I prefer learning about recently discovered plants in the ocean rather than ______ for new types of fish.
   a to search   (b) searching

2 The idea of creatures living on Mars isn't realistic enough ______ searching for them.
   a to continue   b continuing

3 It is less important to find new species ______ it is to save the ones we already know about.
   a then   b than

4 In the future, there will be more jobs in ocean research than ______ space exploration.
   a in   b will be

5 I usually learn more about animals from going to museums ______ I do from watching movies.
   a than   b then

6 There is more water on the surface of the earth ______ land.
   a than   b than is

B **Correct the mistake in each sentence.**

1 She teaches ~~less~~ fewer lessons on space than she does on the ocean.

2 It seems like there is less money available for space exploration then for ocean exploration.

3 Traveling to Mars isn't safe enough justifying sending humans there yet.

4 It's much simpler to explore the ocean then to explore space.

5 The final exam on the stars and the planets was difficult than the English exam.

6 I prefer watching movies about space exploration rather than read about it.

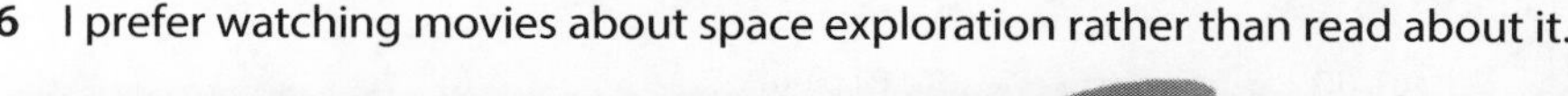

3 GRAMMAR AND VOCABULARY

A **Answer the questions with complete sentences. Explain your answers.**

1 Which is more important: observing the effects of space on humans or finding life on other planets?

____

2 Should scientists focus more on preserving the ocean's environment than on discovering new species?

____

3 Is the International Space Station useful enough to spend government resources on?

____

4 Should more researchers be exploring the earth's oceans?

____

2.2 EXTREME LIFE

1 VOCABULARY: The natural world

A **Cross out the word that is different in meaning.**

1	territory	area	~~border~~
2	sea life	sand	fish
3	plant life	creature	tree
4	origin	creation	destination
5	habitat	environment	pond
6	adaptable	fixed	flexible
7	pond	habitat	lake
8	animal life	volcano	frog

B **Circle the correct word to complete each sentence.**

1 Camels can live for months in the desert without drinking water. They are ______ .
 a plant life b endangered (c) survivors

2 The villagers did not hear the noise from the ______ , but they saw smoke rising in the sky.
 a animal life b volcano c environment

3 Scientists are trying to identify the new ______ they discovered in the river.
 a territory b origin c form of life

4 Cutting down trees in a forest can harm an animal's natural ______ .
 a environment b creature c pond

5 Some berries in the forest are ______ . They can make you very sick.
 a poisonous b plant life c adaptable

6 The Asian elephant is one of the most famous ______ animals. There are fewer than 50,000 of them left on the planet.
 a poisonous b endangered c adaptable

7 Mosquitos are my least favorite ______ . They usually head straight for me even if other people are around.
 a habitats b origins c creatures

2 GRAMMAR: Superlative structures; ungradable adjectives

A **Complete each sentence with a phrase in the box.**

absolutely freezing	completely terrifying	least amount
~~least poisonous~~	most dangerous animals	smallest bird

1 The *least poisonous* snake is called the rat snake. Its bite may hurt, but it isn't deadly.
2 The ______ that scientists have found is called the bee hummingbird.
3 Greenland is one of the coldest places on Earth. It is ______, especially in the winter.
4 Crocodiles are one of the ______ in the world. They kill hundreds of people each year.
5 An active volcano is a/an ______ thing to see.
6 The ______ of sleep a typical adult needs to stay healthy is around six to seven hours per night.

B **Complete the sentences with phrases from the box and your own ideas.**

absolutely awful	most / least adaptable	most / least colorful	most / least dangerous	most / least enjoyable
most / least interesting	most / least pleasant	most / least unique	most / least unlikely	

1 The ______ fish in the ocean is the ______.
2 Places with a lot of sun are the ______ places to live.
3 ______ are one of the ______ insects on Earth.
4 ______ are one of the ______ animals to see in their natural habitat.
5 The ______ animal in the world is the ______.
6 The ______ threat to endangered animals is ______.

3 GRAMMAR AND VOCABULARY

A **Complete the sentences about three of the life forms in the box. Use vocabulary from exercises 1A and 1B, superlative structures, and ungradable adjectives.**

cockroaches	great white shark	kangaroos
king cobra	~~octopus~~	

1 *The octopus is the strangest and most beautiful form of sea life.*
2 ______
3 ______
4 ______

2.3 FINDING OUT

1 LISTENING

A 2.01 **What activities are the people in the photos doing? What is the same about the two activities? What is different? Listen to the conversation and check your answers.**

B 2.01 LISTEN FOR DETAILS **Listen to the conversation again. Complete the sentences with the correct number.**

1 As a beginner, Felix will most likely dive in about ________ meter(s) of water.

2 A scuba diving oxygen tank lasts for ________ hour(s).

3 There are ________ steps to getting certified for scuba diving.

4 Felix will have to complete ________ dive(s) as part of his certification process.

2 CRITICAL THINKING

A THINK CRITICALLY **How do you think scuba diving could be beneficial to the environment? How could it be dangerous to the environment?**

____

____

____

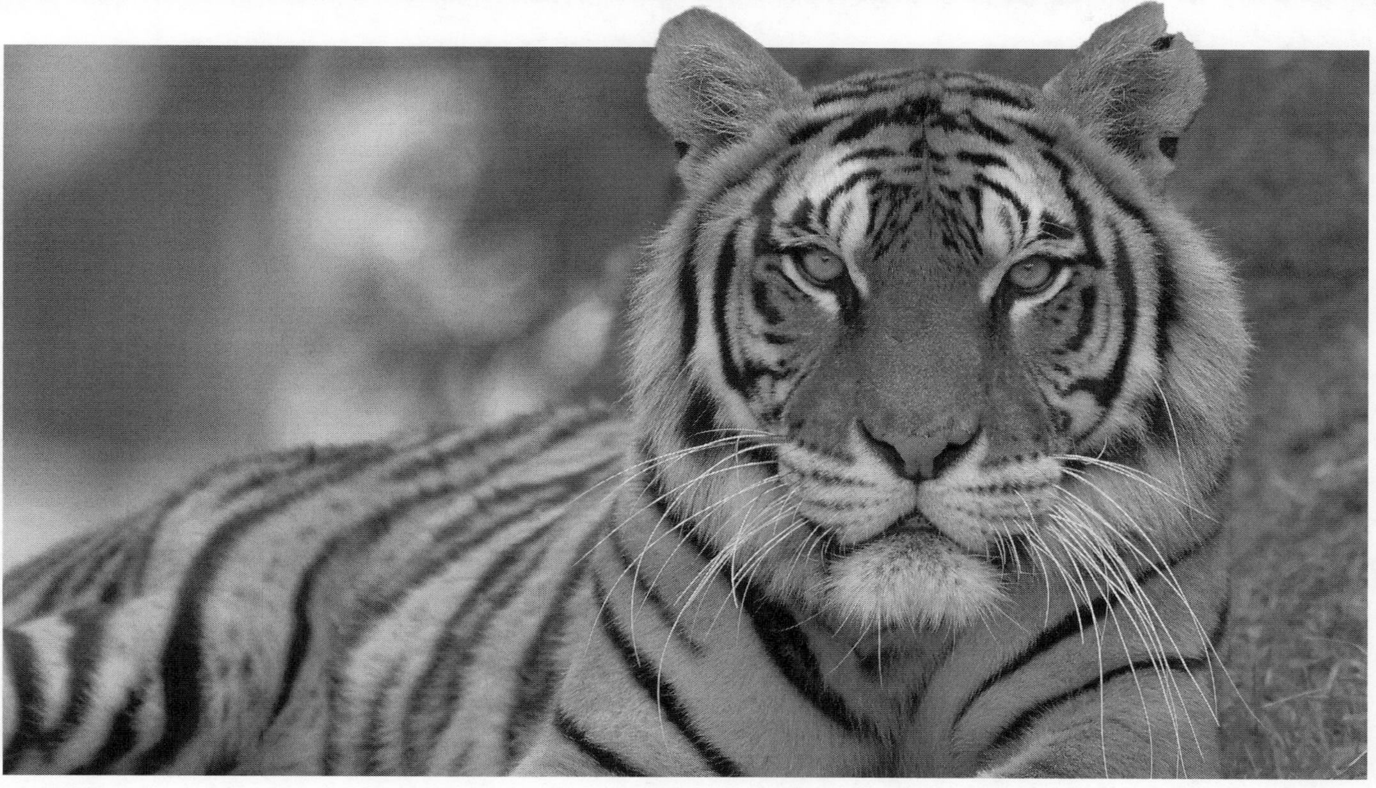

3 SPEAKING

A **Underline the expressions that ask for or provide specific information in each of the sentences below. Then match the questions to the answers.**

1 What exactly do you mean by saying tigers are endangered? ______
2 Is there any danger of the earth being overpopulated someday? ______
3 Would you recommend living in a desert climate? ______
4 Will tourists travel to space someday? ______
5 Is there a risk of injury when scuba diving? ______

a Maybe. One thing to keep in mind is the lack of rain.
b No. First and foremost, it will be too expensive.
c A small one, but it's generally a safe activity.
d There is a risk they will no longer exist someday.
e Yes, some experts say it will happen by the year 2050.

B **Read the situation below. Write three questions and then give three pieces of information. Remember to use phrases for exchanging information.**

Think of a city you've never been to but would like to go to. Imagine you are planning a trip to that city. You have a friend who recently went there, and you want to ask your friend for information. Write three questions you want to ask.

1 ______
2 ______
3 ______

Now, imagine your friend wants to visit a city you know. What three pieces of information would you give to your friend?

1 ______
2 ______
3 ______

2.4 EXTREME LIVING

1 READING

A **Look at the picture. Why do people like to watch survival reality shows? Read the article from an entertainment blog. Does it mention your ideas?**

Home Shows About

ONLY THE STRONG SURVIVE—And Get Paid For It

Why do we watch television shows where people are obviously uncomfortable? For about the last ten years, shows based on surviving in extreme environments have become very popular. In fact, there are currently more than 50 survival reality shows on television around the world.

These shows usually follow a basic structure. A group of strangers is dropped off in a remote location with limited, or no, supplies. They have to find food, water, and a safe place to sleep each night. Every week, the people on the show vote to remove one member of the group. The last remaining survivor usually wins money and prizes, sometimes up to $1 million.

Sometimes, there are only two people rather than a large group. They are allowed to select one tool, such as a sharp knife or something to help start a fire. They then have three weeks to walk to a new location, where food, water, and a ride home will be waiting for them. This becomes a lesson in working as a team and being patient under extreme circumstances.

Locations for survival reality shows are usually extreme; for example, the jungles of Micronesia, where the average annual rainfall is 100 to 200 inches (2540–5080 mm). The temperatures often reach over 100°F (38° C). One thing to keep in mind in these tropical climates is insects. People usually wake up with enormous mosquito bites, which add to other physical problems such as hunger and thirst.

Perhaps we watch these programs because we want to see how far people can push themselves, or we want to watch others have adventures that we'll never experience. Maybe we want to see them succeed, or maybe we're hoping they'll fail. Whatever the reason, it looks like people will be watching survival reality shows for a long time!

B **UNDERSTAND NUMERICAL WORDS AND PHRASES** **Read the article again. Read the statements. Then write *T* (true) or *F* (false).**

1 There are approximately 50 survival reality shows on television. ______
2 Contestants often win more than $1 million. ______
3 It usually rains up to 100 inches per year in Micronesia. ______
4 Temperatures might be higher than 100°F some days. ______

2 CRITICAL THINKING

A **THINK CRITICALLY** **Read the article again. What kind of information do the numbers in the text give?**

______

______

______

3 WRITING

A **USE NUMERICAL WORDS AND PHRASES Think of a city or town that you would like to visit. Answer the questions about the place you chose. You will need to look up some information online.**

1 What is the population?

____

2 What is the average yearly rainfall?

____

3 What is the average yearly snowfall?

____

4 Describe the range of temperatures.

____

5 Describe the environment.

____

B **Write a paragraph that describes the place you chose in exercise 3A. Use numerical words and phrases, and noun + *-like*. Explain why you would like to visit and what makes it interesting.**

____

____

____

____

____

____

____

____

____

CHECK AND REVIEW

Read the statements. Can you do these things?

UNIT 2	Mark the boxes. ☑ I can do it. ? I am not sure. **I can …**	If you are not sure, go back to these pages in the Student's Book.
VOCABULARY	☐ **describe space and ocean exploration.** ☐ **talk about life forms in the natural world.**	page 12 page 14
GRAMMAR	☐ **use comparative structures.** ☐ **use superlative structures and ungradable adjectives.**	page 13 page 15
LISTENING AND SPEAKING SKILLS	☐ **listen for details.** ☐ **use expressions to exchange information.**	page 16 page 17
READING AND WRITING SKILLS	☐ **understand numerical words and phrases.** ☐ **write a description of an area.**	page 18 page 19

UNIT 3 THE WAY I AM

3.1 POWER IN QUIET

1 VOCABULARY: Describing personality

A **Complete each conversation with a phrase in the box.**

attract attention	enjoy the company of	speak softly
speak up	the life of the party	

1 **A** Anna tells great stories about her world travels. People are always fascinated by them.
  B Yeah, she sure is ________________.
2 **A** Why are you sitting in the back of the classroom?
  B I didn't do my homework, so I don't want to ________________ to myself.
3 **A** Can I come to the library with you to study?
  B Sure, but we'll have to ________________ so we don't disturb people.
4 **A** Do you spend time with your co-workers outside of work?
  B Sure. I really ________________ my coworkers. They've become my friends.
5 **A** You have creative ideas. You should ________________ more in meetings.
  B Thanks! That's good advice. I'll try to say more from now on.

B **Circle the correct word to complete each sentence.**

1 Robert wasn't invited to the movies, so he *felt left out / was an introvert.*
2 Each time you *show off / interact with* a native speaker, your English will improve.
3 Even if you're *an extrovert / an introvert*, it's important to spend time with friends to avoid being alone too often.
4 Whenever we go to a party, Jorge loves to *show off / interact with* his dance moves.
5 If I leave my cell phone at home, I'm more likely to *socialize / be reserved*. That way, I meet a lot of new people.
6 At school, Jun chats with his friends a lot. It's obvious he *feels left out / is an extrovert*.

2 GRAMMAR: Relative pronouns; reduced relative clauses

A **Combine the sentences to make one sentence.**

1 Wednesday is one day of the week. I have time to go to my exercise class.
  Wednesday is one day of the week when I have time to go to my exercise class.
2 You can read the book. I bought the book yesterday.
  ____
3 She brought her dog on vacation with her. Her dog's name is Duke.
  ____
4 Valentina invited 50 people to her party. Valentina loves celebrating her birthday with her friends.
  ____
5 I ate lunch at a restaurant. The restaurant was voted the best restaurant in the city.
  ____

B **Circle the correct word to complete each sentence.**

1 My favorite time of year is summer vacation, ______ to a lot of parties.
   a when invited   b which I get invited   (c) when I get invited

2 Some introverts prefer to live in small cities, ______ than large cities.
   a that are less crowded   b which are less crowded   c less crowded

3 My best friend grew up in a small town ______ Friendship.
   a where is called   b which calling   c called

4 People ______ social media often say they enjoy making new friends online.
   a who use   b use   c when they use

5 The speaker, ______ is about the effects of social media, gave an interesting presentation.
   a whose research   b which research   c who research

6 There are many studies ______ being alone too often is bad for a person's health.
   a say   b that say   c that saying

3 GRAMMAR AND VOCABULARY

A **Complete each sentence with a word in the box. You may use a word more than once. Then write a sentence that is true for you using the same relative clause structure.**

called	that	where	~~which~~	who	whose

1 a I like to show off my musical skills, *which* often makes me the life of the party.
   b I like to *show off my cooking skills, which makes me popular with my friends*.

2 a I'm a person ______ enjoys the company of strangers.
   b I'm a person ______.

3 a Being an introvert is a trait ______ should get more respect.
   b Being an introvert ______.

4 a In class, ______ I'm more reserved, I don't speak up very often.
   b In class, ______.

5 a Socializing regularly is an activity ______ I value.
   b Socializing ______.

6 a I'm someone ______ friends are mostly extroverts.
   b I'm someone ______.

7 a All of my classmates liked the information session ______ "How to succeed in college."
   b All of my classmates ______.

B **Write a description of a person you know well. Use relative clauses and words to describe his or her personality.**

3.2 THINGS AND EMOTIONS

1 VOCABULARY: Strong feelings

A **Put the words in the correct places in the chart. You will use one word twice.**

~~bizarre~~	creepy	disgusting	~~fabulous~~	impressive	irritating
satisfying	stunning	tense	uneasy	weird	

Positive	Negative
fabulous	bizarre

B **Circle the correct words to complete the sentences.**

1 Overall, my semester was *stunning* / *satisfying*. I liked my professors and I learned a lot.
2 Animals tend to feel *disgusting* / *uneasy* before natural disasters, such as earthquakes.
3 Almost everyone agrees that her book is *fabulous* / *irritating*. It has won many awards.
4 The floor of the restaurant is *weird* / *disgusting*. There is food and dirt everywhere.
5 Therese feels *tense* / *fabulous* driving at night because she can't see very well.
6 Do you think my dress is *weird* / *uneasy*? I made it myself.
7 Those people in the theater were *impressive* / *irritating*. They talked throughout the entire movie.
8 I used to think broccoli was *creepy* / *gross*, but now it's one of my favorite vegetables.
9 The man's behavior was *bizarre* / *satisfying*, so no one wanted to sit next to him.
10 There is a *stunning* / *creepy* view of the city on top of that building.
11 Anthony gave a/an *weird* / *impressive* speech, which encouraged people to donate money.
12 I love stories about ghosts, even though I find them *satisfying* / *creepy*.

2 GRAMMAR: Present participles

A **Match the sentence halves.**

1 As a manager working at a large corporation, ___c___
2 Some people like to take the bus, ______
3 Today, I'm spending time with my childhood friends, ______
4 Abraham loves to sit on his porch alone, ______
5 The people ______
6 This weekend I'm relaxing, ______
7 The sight of someone ______

a talking about the old days.
b eating makes me hungry.
c Lara works a lot of hours.
d catching up on things I don't have time to do during the week.
e using the time to read or study.
f drinking coffee and enjoying the peace.
g earning the most money donate generously.

B **Complete the sentences with the correct form of the verbs in parentheses.**

1 I get annoyed by ___sitting___ (sit) in traffic, ___waiting___ (wait) for the cars to move.
2 The plane ______ (arrive) from Paris was early, which ______ (make) everyone happy.
3 We ______ (try) the new restaurant, ______ (expect) an excellent meal.
4 As someone ______ (work) in the movie industry, I ______ (watch) a lot of films.
5 The sight of the car ______ (drive) quickly toward me was frightening.
6 She loved ______ (attend) the concert, ______ (listen) to her favorite singer.

3 GRAMMAR AND VOCABULARY

A **Complete the sentences so that they are true for you.**

1 As a child living in ______, I thought ______ was fabulous.
2 As a student studying English, I think ______ is satisfying.
3 It's impressive to dance while ______.
4 Animals eating ______ is disgusting.
5 The sound of people ______ is irritating.

B **Complete the sentences. Use present participles.**

1 ______ makes me uneasy.
2 ______ is stunning.
3 ______ looks bizarre.
4 ______ smells weird.
5 ______ sounds creepy.
6 ______ makes me tense.

3.3 ASKING FOR FAVORS

1 LISTENING

A 3.01 LISTEN FOR INFERENCE **Listen to the conversations. Then answer the questions.**

Conversation 1

1 What does Sam say to show that he's uneasy about taking the personality test?

2 What is the likely relationship between Yulia and Sam?

Conversation 2

3 Do you think Gabrielle has experience in the business world? Why or why not?

4 Do you think Gabrielle is an introvert or an extrovert? Explain your answer.

B 3.01 **Listen to the conversation again. Then answer the questions.**

Conversation 1

1 Why does Sam think he might not be able to help Yulia?

2 What does Yulia say that makes Sam feel better about taking the test?

Conversation 2

3 What does Fernanda say to show she supports Gabrielle's idea to be a health coach?

4 Does Fernanda agree to give Gabrielle money for her business? What does she say?

2 CRITICAL THINKING

A THINK CRITICALLY **What do you think a personality test might reveal about a person? What do you think a personality test might say about you? Would you feel comfortable sharing the results with strangers?**

3 SPEAKING

A **Answer the requests with phrases from the box and your own ideas. More than one answer may be correct. Use each phrase at least once.**

I don't know how much I'd be able to …	I don't mean to be rude, but …
I'd be happy to help you out.	Sorry but I wouldn't be comfortable …
~~Yes, I can probably manage that.~~	

1 **A** Is there any chance you could give me a ride to work tomorrow?
B *Yes, I can probably manage that.* I'll pick you up at 8 a.m.

2 **A** Do you think it would be possible for me to see your notes from class?
B ______ didn't you take your own notes in class today?

3 **A** Would you be willing to lend me some money?
B ______ How much do you need?

4 **A** Is there any chance you could teach me the new software program?
B ______ I don't really know how the new software works.

5 **A** Do you think it would be possible for me to borrow your car?
B ______ lending you my car. I'm usually the only one who drives it.

6 **A** I found a new apartment. Would you be willing to help me move?
B ______ When is your moving date?

B **Complete the conversations with phrases from the box in exercise 3A.**

1 **Boss** Is there any chance you could work late tonight?
Employee ______

2 **Roommate A** Do you think it would be possible for my friend Jack to move in with us?
Roommate B ______

3 **Classmate A** Would you be willing to explain the teacher's lecture to me? I didn't understand most of it.
Classmate B ______

3.4 THE RIGHT JOB FOR ME

1 READING

A **Read the job names in the article. Name one thing a person who works each of the jobs might typically do. Then read the article and check your answers.**

Get Out of Your Comfort Zone at Work

For some people, a typical work day includes sitting at a desk, taking phone calls, and tapping away at a computer. However, there are plenty of more unusual careers for people who want something a little different. Would you like to interact with poisonous snakes, study emoji icons, or eat ice cream all day and get paid for it? Read about three unique jobs and see if they are right for you.

EMOJI TRANSLATOR

Emojis have become so effective in communicating emotions that international corporations now use them to connect with clients. But just as human body language varies across cultures, so do expressions and gestures communicated by emojis. For example, the thumbs-up sign may be positive in the United States, but it is insulting in Russia. Companies are now hiring emoji translators who report on how emojis can cause problems in different cultures.

ICE CREAM TASTER

John Harrison starts his work day at 7:30 a.m. when his taste buds are at their sharpest. He then samples around 20 ice cream flavors, which he analyzes for taste and smell. It's not as easy as it sounds, though. Harrison's formal job title is "flavorologist." People who would like to have this dream-like career should have experience in food science, product development, and maybe even chemistry. They must have an excellent sense of taste, and they may also be responsible for inventing new ice cream flavors.

SNAKE MILKER

Are you uneasy around snakes? Then this job definitely isn't for you. A snake milker extracts poisonous venom from snakes, which is then used to develop treatments for medical conditions. Someone holding this job must be comfortable caring for snakes, making sure they are not harmed in the process. Snake milkers usually have degrees in animal biology, and they may work in research labs, universities, and zoos.

B **IDENTIFY AUDIENCE** **Read the article again. Then answer the questions.**

1 Who is the audience for the text?
   - **a** high school students
   - **b** people who like their jobs
   - **c** people looking for a career change

C **How do you think most readers would feel about each job?**

1 emoji translator ____________________

2 ice cream taster ____________________

3 snake milker ____________________

2 CRITICAL THINKING

A **THINK CRITICALLY** **Would you like to work at any of the jobs mentioned in the article? Why or why not? Is there another unusual job you'd like to have?**

____

____

____

3 WRITING

A Think of *five* words or phrases that describe your personality and give a specific example that illustrates each word or phrase.

B Look online for a job you would be interested in applying for. Think about skills you have that are relevant for the job.

C Write a personal statement for the job you chose in exercise 3B. It should highlight your skills and personality, explaining why they would make you suitable for the job. Use *in order to* in your answer.

CHECK AND REVIEW

Read the statements. Can you do these things?

UNIT 3	Mark the boxes. ☑ I can do it. ? I am not sure. **I can …**	If you are not sure, go back to these pages in the Student's Book.
VOCABULARY	☐ describe personality types. ☐ express things I like and don't like.	page 22 page 24
GRAMMAR	☐ use relative clauses to add description to sentences. ☐ use present participles to describe two events happening at the same time.	page 23 page 25
LISTENING AND SPEAKING SKILLS	☐ listen for inference. ☐ role play making and responding to requests.	page 26 page 27
READING AND WRITING SKILLS	☐ identify audience for a text. ☐ write a personal statement.	page 28 page 29

UNIT 4 COMBINED EFFORT

4.1 IT TAKES A TEAM

1 VOCABULARY: Professional relationships

A **Circle the correct definition of the word in bold.**

1 As a restaurant owner, I **oversee** every aspect of the business.
   (a) watch to make certain something is done correctly
   b ask someone for help or advice
2 Role models, such as famous writers or athletes, often **contribute** to a person's success in life.
   a accept responsibility for
   b give something
3 I couldn't decide which jobs I wanted to apply for, so I **turned to** a career counselor for help.
   a asked someone for help or advice
   b helped someone
4 Frances received a large grant to **assist** her in her research.
   a show or prove that something is true
   b help
5 In order to get the job, Ruth had to **demonstrate** that she could work well on a team.
   a watch to make certain something is done correctly
   b show or prove that something is true

B **Complete the paragraph with the words in the box.**

acts as	build a relationship	build trust
enables us to	~~keep an eye on~~	steer everyone away from

I come from a family with three kids. My sister Annie is the youngest. She's only seven, so we all have to [1] *keep an eye on* her. Monica is the oldest, which means she often [2] ________ our boss, even when our parents are around! I'm in the middle, so it's my job to [3] ________ arguing with each other. Our parents often tell us how important siblings are because we [4] ________ with each one of them, and those relationships will be our models throughout our lives. They also tell us it's important to [5] ________ with each other. That [6] ________ always have people in our lives to rely on.

2 GRAMMAR: Adding emphasis: *so … that*, *such … that*, *even*, *only*

A **Complete the sentences with *even* or *only*.**

1 I ________ need a little more money to buy the car of my dreams.
2 She can speak four languages, ________ Mandarin, which I find really difficult.
3 I'm so busy I don't ________ have time to cook.
4 I ________ trust one person and that's my best friend.
5 The company is growing so fast that their ________ focus is to hire more people.

B **Choose the correct words or phrases to complete each sentence.**

1 It was ______ movie that I left before it was over.

a so scary (b) such a scary

2 She was ______ that she fell asleep on the subway.

a so much tired b so tired

3 Rita ______ has a month to go before she finishes law school.

a only b even

4 Hyun has ______ homework that he has to stay up all night to finish it.

a so much b such

5 I'm ______ that I don't think I'll ever eat again!

a so full b such full

6 The snow was so heavy that I couldn't ______ see where the road was.

a only b even

7 Francis is ______ intelligent that he was accepted to all the best colleges.

a so b such

3 GRAMMAR AND VOCABULARY

A **Use the information to write new sentences. Use the words in parentheses to add emphasis.**

1 Adam's teacher keeps an eye on him at all times. (so … that)

Adam is so lazy in class that his teacher keeps an eye on him at all times.

2 Vera was a good temporary department manager. (such … that)

______

3 My friends steer me away from bad decisions. (only)

______

4 That woman contributes money to the school every year. (so … that)

______

5 Mariah has very little money. She cannot pay the rent. (even)

______

6 I've built a strong relationship with my sister. (such … that)

______

7 It was difficult to demonstrate the new computer system. (so … that)

______

8 I oversee one small department of employees. (only)

______

4.2 DESTRUCTIVE TEAMS

1 VOCABULARY: Assessing ideas

A **Cross out the word that is different in meaning.**

1	valid	~~illegal~~	acceptable
2	destructive	productive	harmful
3	weakness	imperfection	advantage
4	aspect	part	whole
5	point out	hide	tell
6	assess	study	ignore
7	constructive	negative	useful

B **Complete the sentences with the words and phrases in the box.**

consequence	draw attention to
strength	~~think through~~
unreasonable	weigh the pros and cons

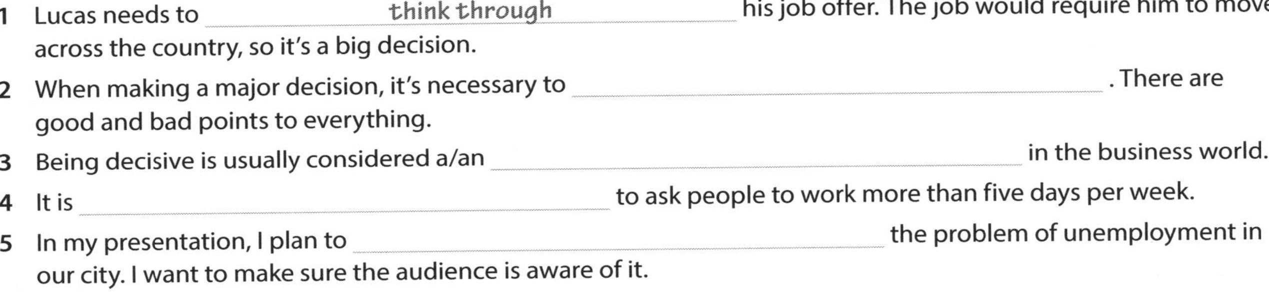

1 Lucas needs to ______think through______ his job offer. The job would require him to move across the country, so it's a big decision.

2 When making a major decision, it's necessary to ____________________ . There are good and bad points to everything.

3 Being decisive is usually considered a/an ____________________ in the business world.

4 It is ____________________ to ask people to work more than five days per week.

5 In my presentation, I plan to ____________________ the problem of unemployment in our city. I want to make sure the audience is aware of it.

6 As a/an ____________________ of missing the final exam, Haewon failed the class.

2 GRAMMAR: Reflexive pronouns; pronouns with *other/another*

A **Circle the correct form of *other/another*.**

1 I got to the restaurant before everyone else. *The others / The other* hadn't arrived yet.
2 Every successful relationship requires respecting *one another / the other.*
3 Our team is too small to get the job done. We need *other / another* person.
4 I have two sisters. One is a lawyer and *the other / another* is a judge.
5 When the *other / others* arrive, we'll begin the meeting.

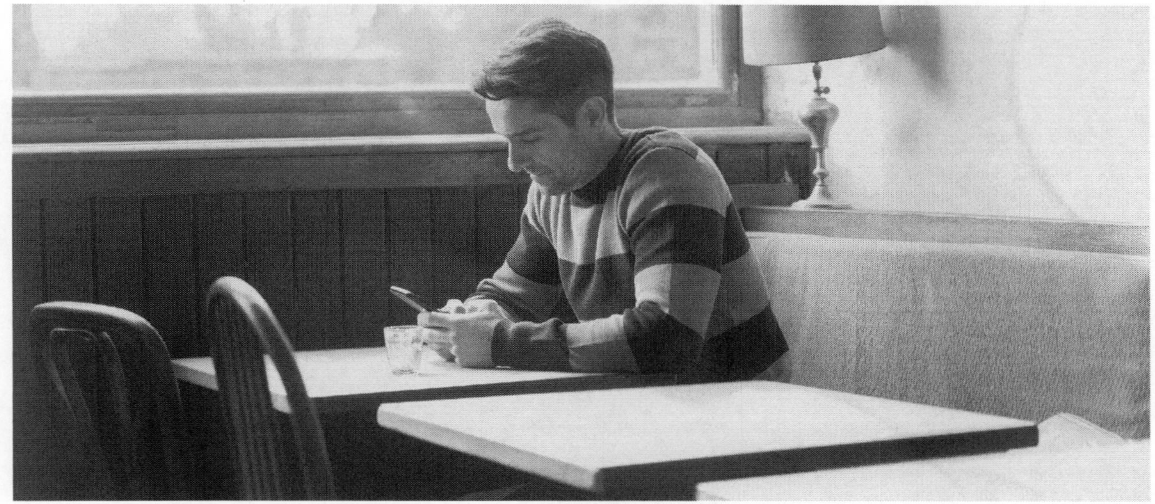

B **Complete the sentences with a reflexive pronoun.**

1 Before you say yes, ask ___yourself___ if you really want to take on another project.
2 He enjoys going to the movies by ______________ .
3 Our team won the championship. We should be proud of ______________ .
4 The computer will shut ______________ down in one hour.
5 She finally bought ______________ a new car.
6 Are you and Dana going to leave ______________ enough time to finish the project?
7 Before looking for a new job, he asked ______________ what his strengths and weaknesses were.

3 GRAMMAR AND VOCABULARY

A **Answer the questions with information so that is true for you. Use complete sentences. Use reflexive pronouns, pronouns with *other/another*, and vocabulary from exercises 1A and 1B.**

1 When are the opinions of others more valid than your own opinions?

____

____

2 How can spending too much time by yourself have negative consequences?

____

____

3 Has another person ever told you that you were being unreasonable?

____

____

4 When was the last time you had to really think something through?

____

____

4.3 TWO PEOPLE, ONE JOB

1 LISTENING

A 4.01 LISTEN FOR ATTITUDE **Listen and answer the questions.**

1 What attitude does Katrina have?
 a helpful b happy c negative
2 What attitude do the audience members have?
 a angry b positive c concerned
3 How certain is Katrina that her company retreat will be successful?
 a very certain b partly certain c not very certain
4 How does Katrina respond to the audience's questions?
 a with doubt b with reassurance c with impatience

B 4.01 **Listen again. Circle the correct answer.**

1 Katrina's company offers:
 a one-day retreats b seven-day retreats (c) a variety of retreats
2 Katrina points out that employees on retreats might worry about:
 a being bored b their schedule c their clients
3 According to Katrina, the benefits of retreats include:
 a playing games b building trust c missing work
4 Katrina helps with:
 a scheduling b looking after other clients c having fun

2 CRITICAL THINKING

A THINK CRITICALLY **Make a list of the advantages and disadvantages of a company retreat. What are some games or activities that would help build relationships at a company retreat?**

3 SPEAKING

A **Put the conversation in order.**

_____ **A** Oh, no. I'd be concerned that I would get lost if I traveled by myself.

_____ **B** That's right, Angela. I'm leaving in a few weeks. I'll be gone for six months.

_____ **B** Well, the upside is that it makes you independent. If you get lost, you just figure it out on your own.

_____ **A** Aren't you worried about being lonely? Or bored?

_____ **A** That's true. I guess I have some unreasonable fears. I'm so worried about everything that I doubt I would have a good time. Well, have fun!

__1__ **A** Hi, Adrian. I heard you were planning to take a trip to South America by yourself.

_____ **B** No, not at all. The main benefit of traveling alone is that it's easy to build relationships with other travelers. Have you ever traveled alone?

B **Write a dialogue in which you try to convince your boss to let you do one of the following: take a year off to study a language abroad, work from home, or give you a raise. Use expressions for discussing advantages and disadvantages.**

You ____

____

Your boss ____

You ____

____

Your boss ____

You ____

____

Your boss ____

4.4 THE ME TEAM

1 READING

A **Think of three benefits that playing team sports might have for children. Then read the article and check your ideas.**

Sports for Life

Team sports have the potential to play a vital role in a child's life. Of course, there are the health benefits that exercise brings. An active child is overall a happier, healthier child. Another plus is that sports expose children to the value of working on a team. They learn to solve problems better, and they build relationships with others. This aspect of team sports is important later in life, too, when they're ready to enter the workforce.

You might say that the downside of team sports is the possibility of losing. In fact, losing contributes to important life skills, too. Everyone loves to celebrate when their team wins. But imagine if your child's team has practiced and worked hard and is confident they're going to win the next game, but they end up losing. That would be a real disappointment, wouldn't it?

But that loss demonstrates to your child that a person can work hard at something and still not succeed. Children learn to keep trying and not to give up. They keep hoping for a more successful outcome. After all, losing isn't a weakness; it's an opportunity for improvement. It also teaches children to share their disappointment with their teammates, so they don't have to take on those negative feelings all by themselves.

Parents often worry about the downside of team sports. They argue that sports can take up a lot of time that their child could spend on academics. However, athletes actually do better in school. Because games like soccer, baseball, and football have specific and complicated rules, memorization and repeated practice are required. These are skills that carry over into learning a language, for example when you weigh the pros and cons, it's obvious that team sports are the clear winner.

B UNDERSTAND AUTHOR'S ATTITUDE **Read the article again. Then answer the questions.**

1 What is the author's attitude toward team sports?

a encouraging **b** pessimistic **c** undecided

2 Find three reasons to support your answer to Question 1.

1 ______

2 ______

3 ______

C **Read the article again. Answer the questions.**

1 What are three benefits of team sports that the author gives? ______

2 What does losing teach children? ______

3 How do team sports help a child's academic performance? ______

2 CRITICAL THINKING

A THINK CRITICALLY **Do you think that the benefits of children playing team sports outweigh the challenges? Why or why not?**

______

3 WRITING

A **Read the summary. Cross out the sentences that don't belong. Why don't the sentences belong in the summary?**

I recently read a book about a young man who grew up in the South of the United States. It was a true story. The author wrote about growing up in poverty and how it was a difficult life for him and his family. It also affected his performance in school. His grades suffered, and he almost dropped out of high school. I am glad his teachers helped him stay in school. He must have had good teachers who cared about him. The author finally graduated from high school and went on to college. While in college, he took a part-time job and was able to buy a car. When he graduated from college, he had excellent grades and he decided to go to law school. I don't know if I could ever finish law school because it sounds very difficult. After law school, he got a job and made enough money to help support his family. He felt very proud of the accomplishments he made in his life, even though it was a hard life at first.

B SUMMARIZE MAIN POINTS **Write a summary of the article on page 32. Decide if it's more appropriate to use *state* or *say* when you report the author's words.**

CHECK AND REVIEW

Read the statements. Can you do these things?

UNIT 4	Mark the boxes. ☑ I can do it. ? I am not sure. **I can …**	If you are not sure, go back to these pages in the Student's Book.
VOCABULARY	☐ **describe supportive people.** ☐ **use words and phrases to assess ideas.**	page 34 page 36
GRAMMAR	☐ **use expressions that add emphasis.** ☐ **use reflexive pronouns and forms of *other/another*.**	page 35 page 37
LISTENING AND SPEAKING SKILLS	☐ **listen for a speaker's attitude.** ☐ **discuss advantages and disadvantages.**	page 38 page 39
READING AND WRITING SKILLS	☐ **understand an author's attitude.** ☐ **summarize main points.**	page 40 page 41

UNIT 5 THE HUMAN FACTOR

5.1 IMITATING REALITY

1 VOCABULARY: Dealing with emotions

A **Complete the sentences with the words and phrases in the box.**

anxiety level | are rational | breathing technique | cure | ~~overcome a fear~~ | try a therapy

1 When you *overcome a fear*, you are no longer afraid of something.
2 When you ______ an illness, you make it better.
3 When your ______ is high, you feel nervous and upset.
4 When you ______, you can think about and explain things clearly.
5 When you are using a(n) ______, you might count your breaths.
6 When you ______, you should talk to an expert.

B **Circle the words or phrases to complete the sentences.**

1 When you *panic* / *calm down* (circled) you feel more relaxed.
2 You might *cure an illness* / *panic* when you take a test.
3 If you are *scared to death* / *conscious* of taking risks, you probably won't start a business.
4 If you *try a therapy* / *regain control*, you have power.
5 When you *overcome a fear* / *are conscious* of something, you are aware of it.
6 Usually, people *are in control* / *regain control* of their actions.

2 GRAMMAR: Real conditionals

A **Match the sentence halves.**

1 If you want to do yoga at home, *c*
2 When patients need medical advice at home, ____
3 My anxiety level becomes very high ____
4 I might take away my son's tablet ____
5 If you want to meet tomorrow, ____
6 I usually regain control of my emotions ____
7 Whenever I see a scary movie, ____
8 If I can't get over my fear of spiders, ____

a if he spends too much time online.
b I can't sleep at night.
c you could watch some videos.
d when I breathe deeply a few times.
e I may see a therapist.
f some doctors will talk to them on Skype.
g whenever I see a snake.
h you'll have to come to my office.

B **Check (✓) the correct sentences. Correct the incorrect sentences.**

1 If you're scared to death of something, listening to music might help you calm down. ✓

2 If I ~~will~~ decide to try a new therapy, I'll ask you to recommend a therapist. ☐

If I decide to try a new therapy, I'll ask you to recommend a therapist.

3 I use a breathing technique when my anxiety level was too high. ☐

4 When ever I panic about something, I imagine I am at the beach relaxing. ☐

5 If I can overcome my fear of crowded places, when I will go to the concert. ☐

6 When you will calm down maybe you'll be more rational. ☐

7 I might try to run a marathon if I can regain control of my health. ☐

8 Whenever I used my meditation app, I am more in control of my thoughts. ☐

9 When you're conscious of the source of your fear, it's easier to overcome it. ☐

10 Whenever I can cure my fear of heights, I may climb Mount Everest. ☐

3 GRAMMAR AND VOCABULARY

A **Read the situations below and give three suggestions for each one. Use real conditionals and the words in the boxes.**

1 Your friend dreams of going hiking in the jungles of Indonesia. However, your friend is terrified of snakes, and Indonesia is home to many poisonous snakes.

~~be scared to death~~	calm down	overcome a fear

a *If you are scared to death, try to think of something positive instead.*

b

c

2 Your friend tells you that every time he goes to a party, he feels anxious. He is nervous meeting new people.

be conscious of	be in control of	breathing technique

a

b

c

3 Your classmate is very intelligent, but she freezes every time she takes a test. She ends up getting a low grade.

anxiety level	panic	try a therapy

a

b

c

5.2 THE END OF THE OFFICE?

1 VOCABULARY: Willingness and unwillingness

A **Circle the correct words to complete the sentences.**

1 Alexandra ______ work at home because she doesn't think she would get a lot of work done.
   a is eager to   (b) is reluctant to
2 Morgan ______ be his own boss. He likes making his own schedule and not having to explain his actions to anyone.
   a is more than happy to   b has no desire to
3 I ______ communicate with coworkers via text message because I don't want to share my cell phone number.
   a am unwilling to   b have no intention of
4 Alisha doesn't like to wake up early. She ______ change her work schedule.
   a hesitates to   b is dying to
5 If an employee ______ driving to work every day, he or she might look for a job that involves working from home.
   a is passionate about   b is against
6 When starting your own business at home, you have to ______ separate your work time from your leisure time, so that you don't work too much.
   a be prepared to   b be anxious to

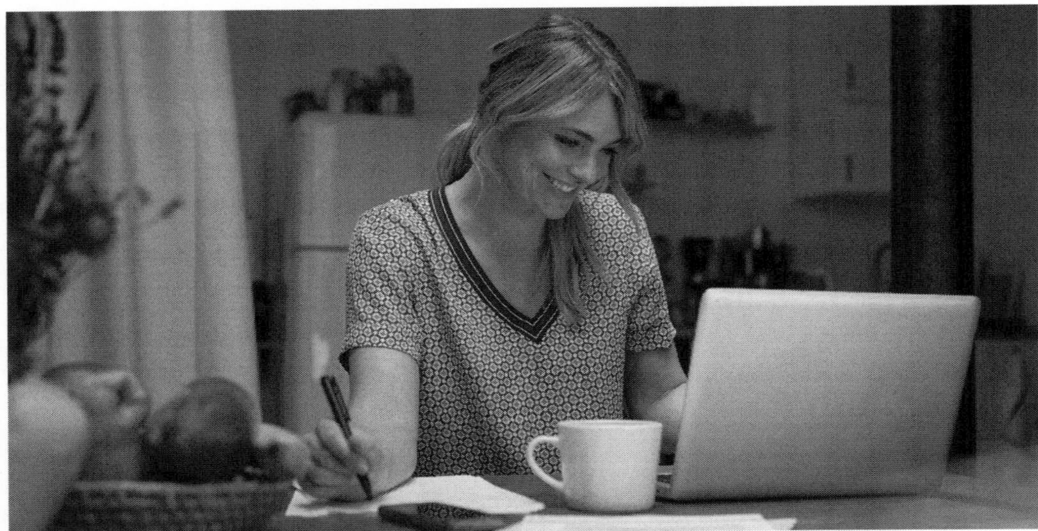

2 GRAMMAR: Conditionals: alternatives to *if*

A **Circle the correct words or phrases to complete the sentences.**

1 We can have our meeting via video call (*as long as*) / *unless* the internet connection is strong.
2 My boss said I can work at home *even if* / *providing* I come into the office once a month.
3 A company is successful *only if* / *even if* the employees are happy and productive.
4 I won't work from home *unless* / *providing that* I move to a bigger house.
5 I don't mind working in an office *even if* / *provided that* I can set my own schedule.
6 I love working at home and wouldn't go back to an office, *so long as* / *even if* you paid me more money.
7 I will invest in your business, but *only if* / *unless* you give me a percentage of your profits.
8 You can take a long vacation *unless* / *so long as* you finish your work before you go.

B **Complete the conversation in a job interview between the interviewer (A) and the candidate (B). Use the correct form of the phrases in parentheses.**

1 **A** ___Are___ you ___eager to___ work here? *(be eager to)*

2 **B** Yes. I ______ the work your company does. I want to work here even if I have to start at an entry level position. *(be passionate about)*

3 **A** ______ you ______ socialize outside of work, provided that it's an event that helps build relationships with your coworkers? *(be willing to)*

4 **B** Sure, I ______, so long as I don't have to stay out too late. *(be more than happy to)*

A Do you plan to continue your training in this field? For example, do you have any intention of getting a master's degree?

5 **B** Well, I ______ say yes to that because school is very expensive. I'd like to continue my training, but only if there was financial assistance. *(hesitate to)*

6 **A** If you work here, you will share an office with several of your coworkers. ______ you ______ that? *(be against)*

B That's fine with me. I don't mind sharing an office.

A Great! Are you ready to start work immediately?

7 **B** Yes, I ______ start tomorrow as long as you want to hire me. *(be prepared to)*

3 GRAMMAR AND VOCABULARY

A **Complete the sentences with your own ideas.**

1 I'm reluctant to go back to school even if ___my job pays for it___.

2 I'm eager to travel to foreign countries so long as ______.

3 I hesitate to find a new job unless ______.

4 I'm more than happy to help you with your problem, providing ______.

5 I have no desire to go to the gym unless ______.

6 I'm anxious to learn how to drive even if ______.

5.3 STOP BLAMING GAMING

1 LISTENING

A 🔊 5.01 LISTEN FOR SPEAKER'S DEGREE OF CERTAINTY **Listen to the podcast about banning technology in the home. Is the speaker certain or uncertain about his or her ideas? Listen to the language describing these ideas and check (✓)the ones that sound confident.**

☐ 1 **Ingrid** So yes, spending too much time online can lead to problems in a child's emotional development.

☐ 2 **Ingrid** Parents simply need to be conscious of how much time is spent online.

☐ 3 **Host** Their home is absolutely free of modern technology.

☐ 4 **Leon** You can bet those parents have inside knowledge about how companies make sure that kids want to use devices all the time.

☐ 5 **Leon** But who knows how long that calmness lasts?

B 🔊 5.01 **Listen to the podcast again. Then answer the questions.**

1 Why did Leon ban technology in his home?

2 What is 27% more likely to happen when teenagers use social media too often?

3 Why did Leon say the parents have "inside knowledge?" What is their "inside knowledge?"

4 What alternative does Ingrid suggest to a total technology ban?

5 How does Leon feel about a "no-tech" week?

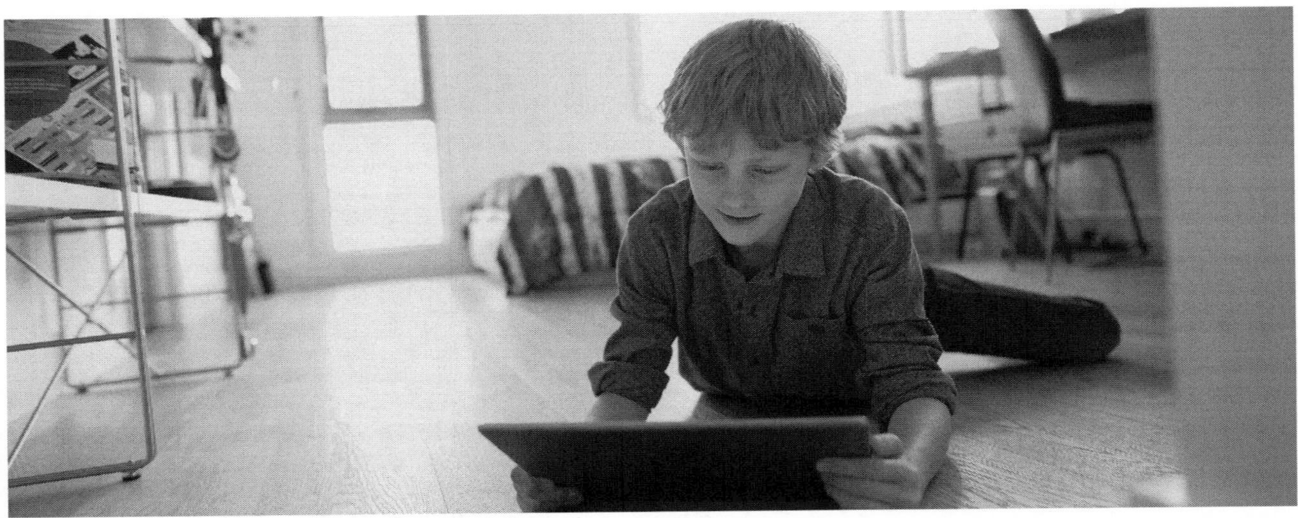

2 CRITICAL THINKING

A THINK CRITICALLY **Whose view about banning technology in the home do you agree with the most? Why?**

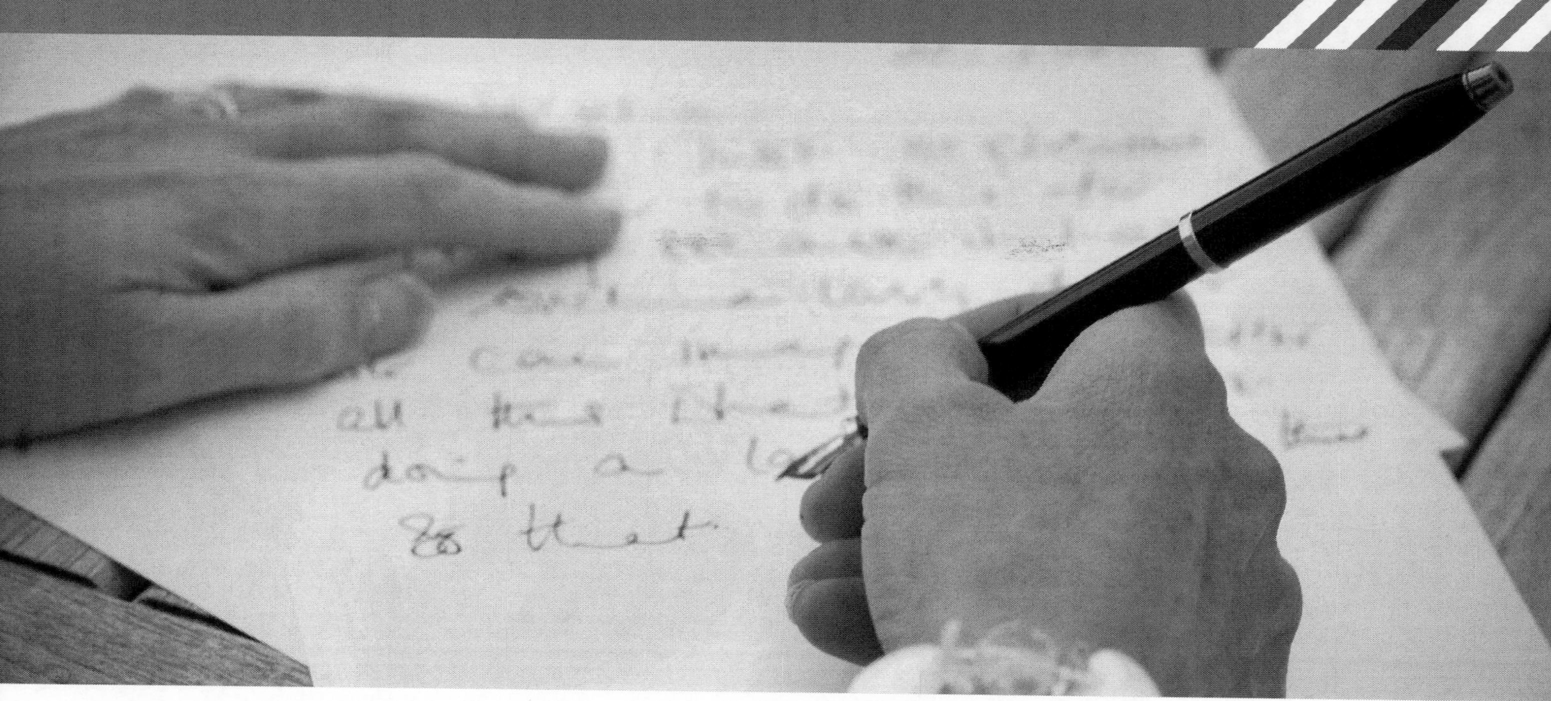

3 SPEAKING

A **Complete the conversation with the expressions in the box. More than one answer may be correct.**

at the same time	I don't have a clue	I guarantee that	it's a well-known fact
on the contrary	that said	Who knows	you can bet that

Thomas I'm going on a complete digital detox. I'm not going to use anything internet-based for 30 days. [1] I guarantee that I'll be more focused afterwards.

Ivan Well, [2] ________ that too much screen time before bed negatively affects a person's sleep, so you'll also be more rested.

Thomas Exactly. And I'll have more free time. [3] ________ ? Maybe I'll learn a language or a musical instrument.

Ivan [4] ________ , you might have *too* much free time. How do you plan to stay in touch with people?

Thomas [5] ________ . I guess writing letters is a thing of the past. [6] ________ , it might be a good way to connect with people more deeply.

Ivan [7] ________ it'll be tough at times. [8] ________ , I don't think I could ever do it, and I respect you for trying.

B **Write a contrasting answer to each statement. Use the expressions from exercise 3A.**

1 When teenagers use social media too often, their risk of depression increases.
At the same time, it can be a good way to help shy kids interact with others.

2 People would be much happier if they didn't have to drive to their offices every day.
____

3 If people work at home, they may become lonely.
____

4 I guarantee that kids will complain if they can't use technology for one week.
____

5 I don't have a clue how you can work in the technology industry and not use technology.
____

5.4 WHAT LANGUAGE BARRIER?

1 READING

A **Read the article. Underline the formal and informal connecting expressions. As an article on a blog, should it be more formal?**

CULTURAL ETIQUETTE IN THE DIGITAL AGE

When we think of language barriers while traveling, one of the first images that we often think of is a lost traveler, gesturing wildly to a confused local person.

The lost traveler doesn't know the local language, nor does he or she understand that gestures can be culture-based, too. In the last decade or so, another barrier to being understood in a new culture has appeared—cell phone etiquette.

OK, imagine this situation. An American man is on the subway in Japan when his cell phone rings. He answers and has a brief conversation. He keeps his voice low, but he still senses that people are annoyed. Later, he learns that it's actually rude to talk on a cell phone in public places in Japan. There's not much he can do to correct his previous poor behavior, so the next time he rides the subway, he simply switches his phone to silent.

Cell phone use can cause problems in the same way a misunderstood word or gesture can. And in the same way, knowing the correct action depends on which culture you're dealing with.

Trying to catch up on phone calls during lunch? If you're eating, you'll be considered rude if the person on the other end is from the United Kingdom. Therefore, save your UK calls for after lunch.

With regards to answering calls in public places, it's acceptable in the United States; however, it's rude if you're in the middle of a face-to-face conversation. In China, on the other hand, you may be in for a surprise if your in-person conversation is interrupted when your friend takes a call from another person.

It's easy to create cultural barriers. That said, the best way to avoid them is to educate yourself whenever dealing with cultures different from your own.

GLOSSARY

etiquette (n) the set of rules or customs that control accepted behavior in particular social groups or social situations

gesture (n) the movement of the hands, arms, or head to express an idea or feeling

B **UNDERSTAND PROBLEMS AND SOLUTIONS** **Read the article again. How did the person on the subway in Japan correct his error?**

....

....

C **Read the article again. Circle the correct answer.**

1 When it comes to cell phones:
   - a etiquette is similar in most countries.
   - b something rude in one culture may be acceptable in another.
   - c it's alright to follow the culture you are from, no matter which country you're in.

2 The writer uses the example of the lost traveler to show that:
   - a everyone should speak a foreign language.
   - b everyone gets lost when they travel.
   - c not knowing language and etiquette can cause problems.

3 What effect does the phrase, "OK, imagine this" have?
   - a It asks the reader to picture a situation.
   - b It asks the reader to agree with a situation.
   - c It asks the reader to think of another example.

2 CRITICAL THINKING

A **What is your opinion of using cell phones in a public place? In what situations do you think this is acceptable or not acceptable?**

____

____

____

3 WRITING

A **Read the statements. Underline the organizing and connecting expressions. Then write *O* if it's an opinion and *F* if it's a fact.**

1 With regards to cell phones, children in the United States get their first one around age ten, on average. ___
2 That said, speaking loudly on a cell phone in public is rude. ___
3 So yes, cell phone etiquette varies from country to country. ___
4 As for the increased use of cell phones, Finland was the first country to have more cell phones than landlines. ___
5 OK, cell phones are a necessary part of life. ___

B STATE OPINION AND GIVE EXAMPLES **Write a paragraph about the use of cell phones in public. Give examples of times when it could be a problem, and how that problem could be solved. Use organizing and connecting expressions when possible.**

____

____

____

____

____

____

CHECK AND REVIEW

Read the statements. Can you do these things?

UNIT 5	Mark the boxes. ☑ I can do it. ? I am not sure.		If you are not sure, go back to these pages in the Student's Book.
		I can …	
	VOCABULARY	☐ **use phrases to discuss emotions.** ☐ **use phrases to explain willingness and unwillingness.**	page 44 page 46
	GRAMMAR	☐ **use real conditionals for general facts and possible future situations.** ☐ **use conditionals with alternatives to *if*.**	page 45 page 47
	LISTENING AND SPEAKING SKILLS	☐ **listen for phrases that express degrees of certainty.** ☐ **use expressions to discuss and contrast ideas.**	page 48 page 49
	READING AND WRITING SKILLS	☐ **understand problems and solutions.** ☐ **state an opinion.**	page 50 page 51

UNIT 6 EXPECT THE UNEXPECTED

6.1 GOING VIRAL

1 VOCABULARY: Talking about fame

A **Match the sentences.**

1 There are a lot of negative comments about him on gossip websites. d
2 He works hard to tell people about problems in our society. ____
3 His name is on the front page of the newspaper today. ____
4 He will go to the party for a few minutes, but then he has to leave. ____
5 He can sing and dance, and he plays the piano. ____
6 Tens of thousands of people watch his video every week. ____

a He makes headlines.
b It gets hits.
c He raises awareness.
d He has a bad reputation.
e He makes concerts entertaining.
f He will make an appearance.

B **Circle the correct words to complete the sentences.**

1 They asked Colin to *make headlines / do the broadcast* since he was the only person with television experience.
2 You *have never heard of / raise awareness of* someone if you don't know the person's name.
3 You should do something kind if you want to *make an appearance / catch somebody's attention.*
4 In his speech, he plans to *get hits / praise his mother* for helping him succeed.
5 You might *have a good reputation / get publicity* if you do something terrible.
6 She never intended to *seek fame / praise somebody*; however, everyone in the world knows her name.

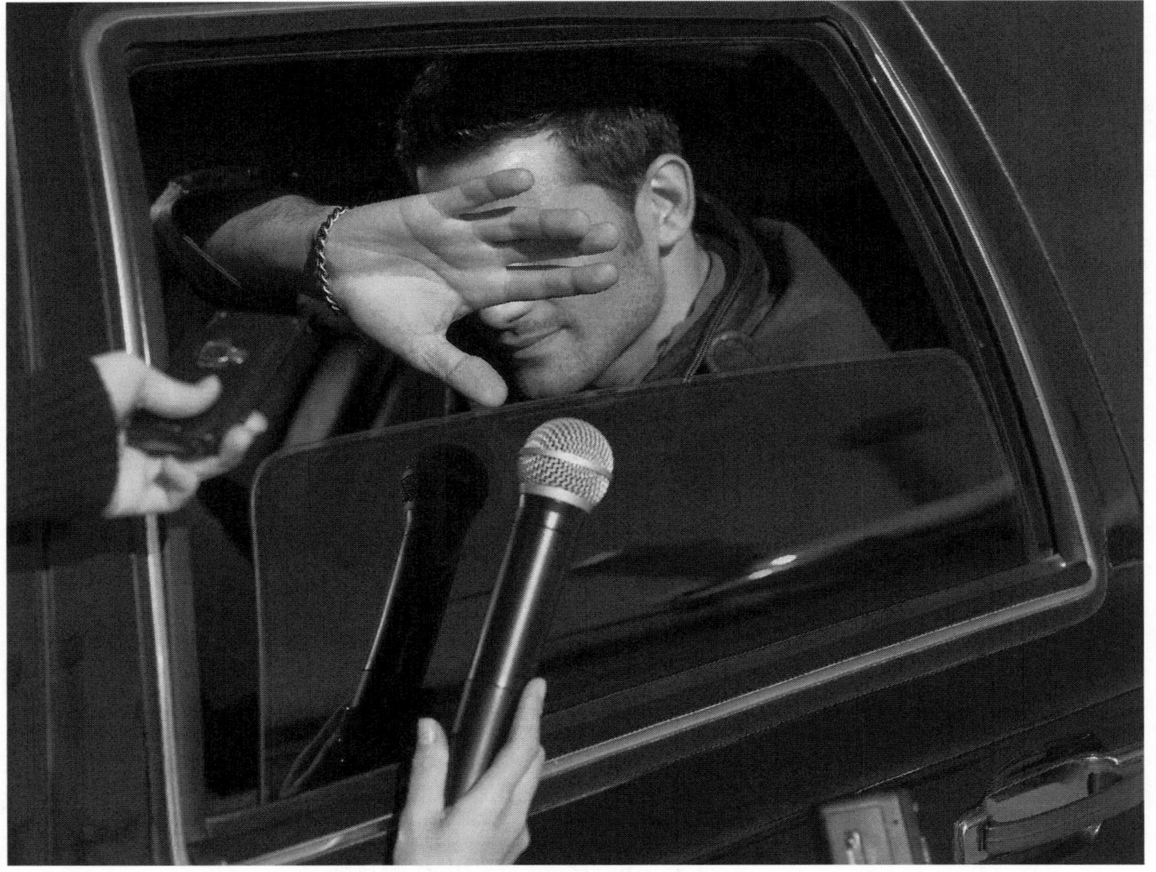

2 GRAMMAR: Narrative tenses

A **Circle the correct words to complete the sentence.**

1 He hadn't ______ for attention when he planned his cross-country bike ride.
   (a) been looking   b been looked   c looks
2 As the man ______ the young girl, several people were recording it on their cell phones.
   a rescuing   b rescued   c had rescued
3 She made her students laugh while she ______ her class.
   a is teaching   b taught   c had taught
4 She had been an actor for ten years before people ______ recognizing her.
   a had started   b start   c started
5 She had been taking care of animals for a long time before her story ______ in the news.
   a appearing   b appeared   c had been appearing
6 People were already talking about her voice as she ______ the song.
   a finishes   b finishing   c finished

B **Underline the event in each sentence that happens first. If the events happen at the same time, write *S* on the line.**

1 When Kiley was growing up, she didn't play any sports. ______
2 In high school, she was trying to get in shape, and she started playing on a basketball team. ______
3 She had been playing for about six months before someone wrote an article about her in a magazine. ______
4 Kylie helped her team win game after game, even though she had only been trying to get in shape. ______
5 Kylie hadn't planned on becoming famous before the article appeared in the magazine. ______
6 From then on, during her athletic career, she encouraged other young girls to play sports, too. ______

3 GRAMMAR AND VOCABULARY

A **Respond to *three* of the statements with information so that is true for you. Use the past continuous, past perfect, or past perfect continuous.**

1 Describe a situation where you or someone you know got a lot of hits on social media.
   My friend had been putting pictures of her food on social media for about a year when she started to get a lot of hits.
2 Describe a time you or someone you know made headlines.
   ______
3 Describe how you caught your parents' attention when you were a child.
   ______
4 Describe a time when someone unexpected made an appearance at a big party or event.
   ______
5 Describe a situation in which you raised awareness of a social issue.
   ______

6.2 NOT AGAIN!

1 VOCABULARY: Reporting verbs

A **Circle the correct definitions.**

1 confirm
  (a) to say that something is true
  b to say that something is strange
2 hope to
  a to want something to happen
  b to say that something is true
3 announce
  a to talk with too much pride about what you have done
  b to tell a group of people about something
4 swear
  a to say that you are sure something is true
  b to pretend you don't know something

B **Cross out the word or phrase that is different in meaning.**

1	propose	suggest	~~remove~~
2	estimate	deceive	guess
3	have doubts about	be uncertain	be certain
4	insist	say firmly	forget
5	deny	accept	oppose

2 GRAMMAR: Reported speech with modal verbs

A **Check (✓) the correct sentences. Correct the incorrect sentences. Sentences should be in the past tense.**

1 I argued that we will need another month to complete the project. ☐
I argued that we would need another month to complete the project.
2 They explained that they might not come to the ceremony. ☐

3 They confirmed that they won't refund my money. ☐

4 We told everyone that they should come to our house early. ☐

5 He said he had doubts that he can show up on time. ☐

B **Rewrite the second line in each conversation as reported speech. Use a variety of reporting verbs.**

1 **Guest** Do you have any rooms available tonight?
Hotel employee No, sorry. We won't have a room free until tomorrow.
The hotel employee claimed they wouldn't have a room free until tomorrow.
2 **Customer** I forgot my wallet, so I'm afraid I can't pay the bill.
Waiter That's OK. You can come back tomorrow and pay.

3 **Mikhail** The subway isn't running. I don't know how I'm going to get to work.
Judi I might be able to help you.

3 GRAMMAR AND VOCABULARY

A **Rewrite the sentences in reported speech using the subject and verb in parentheses. Supply a subject for the sentences if necessary.**

1 "The new smartphones will go on sale next week." (the company / announce)

The company announced that the new smartphones would go on sale next week.

2 "We will arrive in Los Angeles on time." (pilot / claim)

3 "The meeting will start at 9:00 a.m." (my boss / confirm)

4 "I could do a better job if I were given the chance." (the young man / argue)

5 "The bus will not be late." (the driver / insist)

6 "I can make the best chocolate cake in the world." (the chef / boast)

B **Imagine you just moved into a new apartment. When you moved in, you found that the landlord had not done what he promised. Look at the conversation you had with the landlord and the problems below. Report the conversation to a friend. Use reporting verbs from the word box.**

claim	confirm	estimate	explain
insist	say	swear	tell

You Hmm, I don't think I like the bright green walls.

Landlord Oh, that's no problem. I can paint them white before you move in.

You OK. And are the neighbors upstairs noisy?

Landlord Oh, no. They're very quiet. You won't even know they're there!

You Great, but I don't see a refrigerator in the kitchen.

Landlord It's getting repaired and will be here soon. If it takes too long, I might just buy a new one.

You Sounds good. And what about the backyard? Can I use it whenever I want to?

Landlord Sure, it's all yours. You could even have parties and invite your friends.

Problems:

- He didn't paint the walls.
- The neighbors are very noisy.
- There's no refrigerator in the kitchen.
- The backyard is now full of old furniture.

First, the landlord claimed he could paint the walls before I moved in.

6.3 SOMETHING IN THE WATER

1 LISTENING

A **Listen to a conversation between Evelyn and Luisa. How do they know each other?**

a they're neighbors

b they're mother and daughter

c they're close friends

B 6.01 UNDERSTAND MEANING FROM CONTEXT **Listen to the conversation again. Guess the meaning of the words below. What clues helped you to work out their meaning?**

1 biscotti

guess: ______________________

clues: ______________________

2 dunking

guess: ______________________

clues: ______________________

3 love seat

guess: ______________________

clues: ______________________

4 brick and mortar

guess: ______________________

clues: ______________________

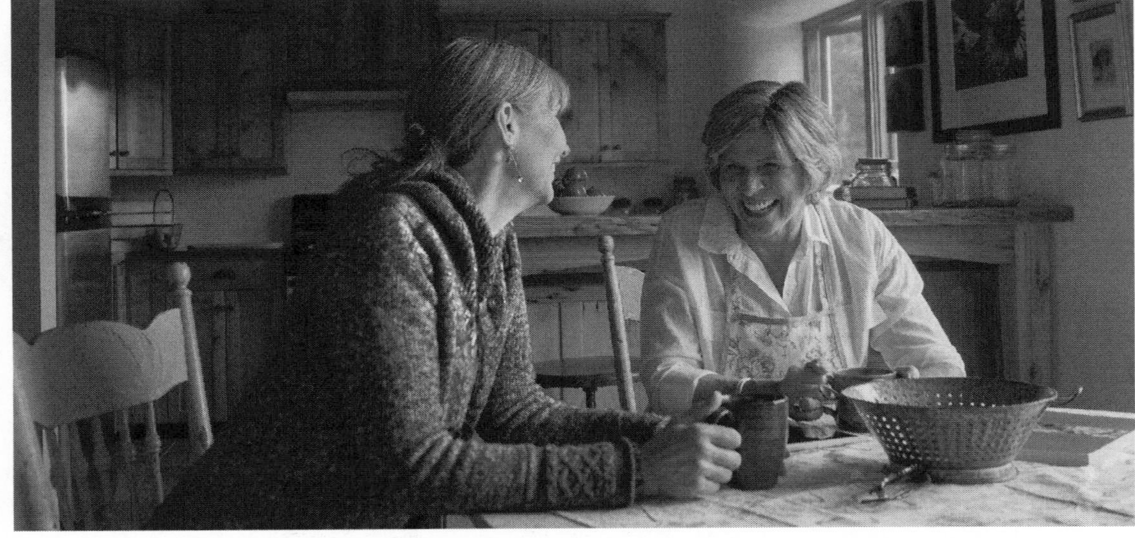

2 CRITICAL THINKING

A THINK CRITICALLY **What makes a good neighbor? Is Evelyn a good neighbor for coming to Luisa's house? Why or why not?**

____

____

____

3 SPEAKING

A **Put the conversation in order.**

_____ **Ben** You must have been hungry.

_____ **Ben** I assume they cancelled the party, and everyone went home.

_____ **Jun** The server brought our food on a tray, but because it was dark, he tripped and all of it went flying across the dining room. We waited another half an hour for new meals.

_____ **Ben** Uh-oh. What?

__1__ **Ben** How was the anniversary party last night?

_____ **Ben** I suppose you fed everyone and saved the party.

_____ **Jun** Not at all. We lit candles, and someone used their smartphone to play music. But then something terrible happened.

_____ **Jun** To an extent, but you know I always have snacks hidden in my bag.

_____ **Jun** It was interesting. Because of the big storm, the power went out. It was totally dark inside the restaurant.

B **Write a short conversation for each situation below.**

1 You went to the airport to catch a flight for a business trip. You arrived on time for your flight, but when you went to check in, you realized you were at the wrong airport. You tell your coworker about it the next day.

You _____

Your coworker _____

You _____

Your coworker _____

You _____

Your coworker _____

You _____

Your coworker _____

2 You were working on a research paper when your computer crashed. You went to the school library to use one of the computers there, but it was closed. Your paper was due the next morning. You tell your classmate about it the next day.

You _____

Your classmate _____

You _____

Your classmate _____

You _____

Your classmate _____

You _____

Your classmate _____

6.4 GETTING IT WRONG

1 READING

A **Read the headline and the first paragraph of the story. What dream do you think came true for the writer? Read the story to check your answer.**

The dream that came true was: ______________________________

____

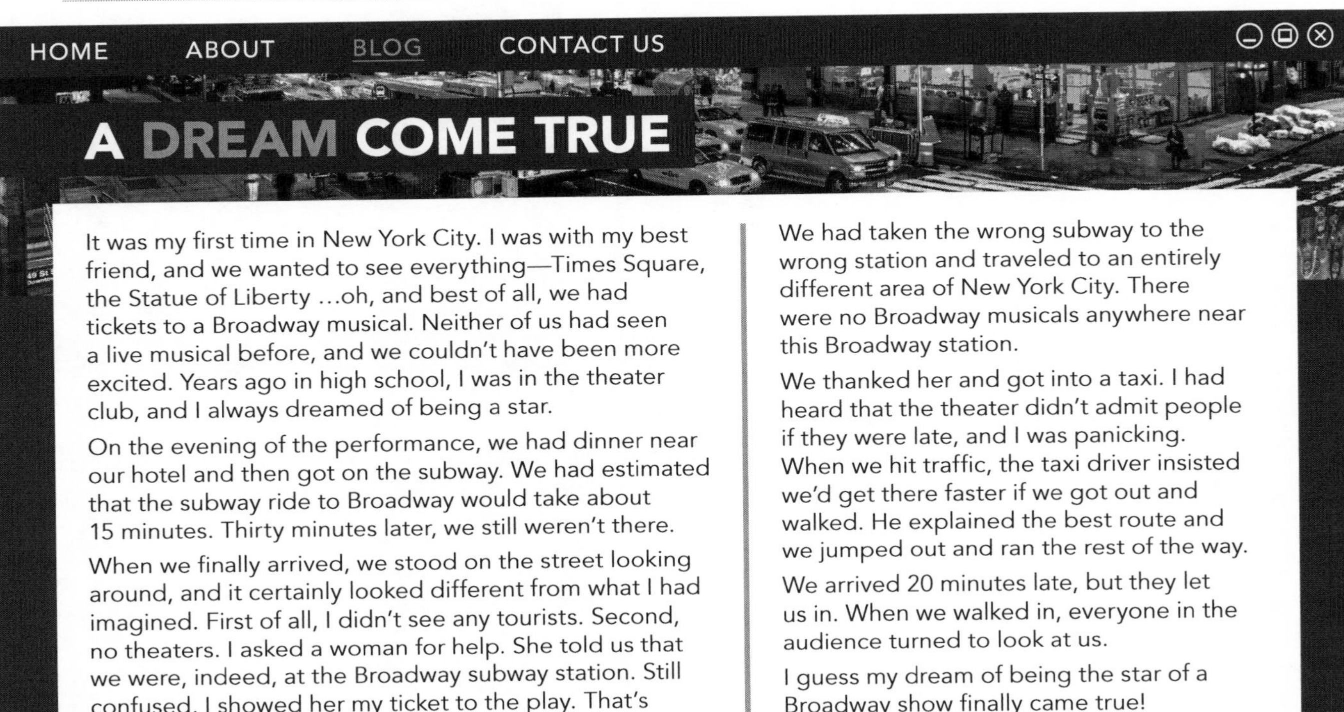

A DREAM COME TRUE

It was my first time in New York City. I was with my best friend, and we wanted to see everything—Times Square, the Statue of Liberty …oh, and best of all, we had tickets to a Broadway musical. Neither of us had seen a live musical before, and we couldn't have been more excited. Years ago in high school, I was in the theater club, and I always dreamed of being a star.

On the evening of the performance, we had dinner near our hotel and then got on the subway. We had estimated that the subway ride to Broadway would take about 15 minutes. Thirty minutes later, we still weren't there.

When we finally arrived, we stood on the street looking around, and it certainly looked different from what I had imagined. First of all, I didn't see any tourists. Second, no theaters. I asked a woman for help. She told us that we were, indeed, at the Broadway subway station. Still confused, I showed her my ticket to the play. That's when it hit her.

We had taken the wrong subway to the wrong station and traveled to an entirely different area of New York City. There were no Broadway musicals anywhere near this Broadway station.

We thanked her and got into a taxi. I had heard that the theater didn't admit people if they were late, and I was panicking. When we hit traffic, the taxi driver insisted we'd get there faster if we got out and walked. He explained the best route and we jumped out and ran the rest of the way.

We arrived 20 minutes late, but they let us in. When we walked in, everyone in the audience turned to look at us.

I guess my dream of being the star of a Broadway show finally came true!

B **UNDERSTAND IRONY** **Read the story. Then answer the questions.**

1 How did the writer realize she had made a mistake?

____

2 What is ironic about the subway station they went to?

____

3 What is ironic about the writer's final sentence?

____

C **Read the story again. Then answer the questions.**

1 In high school, the writer:
- a went to New York City.
- b wanted to be a star.
- c met her best friend.

2 When they got off the subway, the writer assumed:
- a there would be more tourists.
- b they were late for the play.
- c they would be in Times Square.

3 The writer panicked because:
- a the woman gave them the wrong information.
- b the driver told them to get out of the taxi.
- c they might not be let in to the theater.

2 CRITICAL THINKING

A **THINK CRITICALLY** **What do you think the writer and her friend did when the audience turned to look at them? What do you think the audience thought about them?**

____

____

3 WRITING

A **MAKE A STORY INTERESTING** **Read the story again. Underline examples of each of the points below.**

1 A variety of narrative verb tenses in the past.

2 Linking and organizing expressions.

3 Different kinds of sentences: conditionals *(if)*, relative clauses (*who, which*), time clauses (*when, after*), *There was/were*, reported speech, etc.

4 Reporting verbs other than *say*.

5 Two long sentences and two short sentences.

B **Write a story about one of the situations below. Use all of the writing points in exercise 3A to make your story interesting.**

1 Imagine that you and your friend got lost on a desert island for one week. Explain how you ate, where you slept, and how you found your way to safety. Describe some of the things you and your friend said during the week you were lost. ____

____

____

2 Tell a story about a time when you went to a large social event. Describe what people wore, ate, and talked about. ____

____

____

CHECK AND REVIEW

Read the statements. Can you do these things?

UNIT 6	Mark the boxes. ☑ I can do it. ? I am not sure. **I can ...**	If you are not sure, go back to these pages in the Student's Book.
VOCABULARY	☐ **use expressions to talk about fame.** ☐ **use a variety of reporting verbs.**	page 54 page 56
GRAMMAR	☐ **use narrative tenses to tell a story.** ☐ **use reported speech with the correct form of modals.**	page 55 page 57
LISTENING AND SPEAKING SKILLS	☐ **guess the meaning of unfamiliar words from context.** ☐ **use expressions to make, contradict, and clarify. assumptions**	page 58 page 59
READING AND WRITING SKILLS	☐ **identify and understand irony.** ☐ **make a story interesting with a variety of grammar techniques.**	page 60 page 61

1.5 TIME TO SPEAK A step forward

A **Talk to someone you know who is a generation or more older than you (parent, grandparent, teacher, etc.). Try to speak in English, if possible. Take notes in English. Use the questions below to help you.**

- Ask how life was different in the past compared to the present.
- Ask about any new technology he or she witnessed, the type of clothes he or she wore, the different kinds of entertainment, what school was like, and so on.

B **During your next class, discuss your results with a classmate.**

2.5 TIME TO SPEAK Natural limits

A **Search online for outdoor adventure travel companies. Look at a few different websites and identify an outdoor adventure you are interested in. Write down at least three questions you have about your selected trip and research the answers.**

B **Tell a classmate about your activity. Did you have the same questions? How are your activities similar?**

3.5 TIME TO SPEAK The way I am

A **Interview someone who has an interesting job. Interview the person in English, if possible. Take notes. Use the prompts below to help you.**

- Ask the person to describe the job.
- Then ask what qualities a person should have in order to do the job well.

B **During your next class, share your findings with a classmate.**

4.5 TIME TO SPEAK It takes a team

A **Think of or research a list of jobs you could do from home. Write the advantages and disadvantages of working from home.**

Jobs you can do from home	Advantages	Disadvantages

B **Present your ideas in your next class. Compare your ideas with other students.**

5.5 TIME TO SPEAK The human factor

A **Create a survey about cell phone behavior. Think of four or five questions to ask. Give the survey to your family and friends. Use the example questions below to help you.**

Example survey questions

- Do you think it's OK to eat while you're talking on your cell phone?
- What annoys you the most about other people's cell phone behavior?
- Do you use your cell phone when you're in a restaurant? Why or why not?

B **Bring the results to your next class and share them with your classmates. Who had the most interesting survey questions and responses?**

6.5 TIME TO SPEAK Expect the unexpected

A **Prepare to tell a story about one of the topics below. Make some notes. Practice telling your story by saying it out loud. You can also record yourself and listen to your story to see if you want to make any changes.**

Topics:

- the worst haircut I ever received
- the first/last day at my job or at school
- a time when I miscommunicated with someone

B **Tell your story to a friend, family member, or classmate. Ask them if they have a story about a similar topic.**

NOTES

The authors and publishers acknowledge the following sources of copyright material and are grateful for the permissions granted. While every effort has been made, it has not always been possible to identify the sources of all the material used, or to trace all copyright holders. If any omissions are brought to our notice, we will be happy to include the appropriate acknowledgments on reprinting & in the next update to the digital edition, as applicable.

Key: U = Unit.

Photographs
The following photographs are sourced from Getty Images.

U1: Absodels/ABSODELS/Getty Images Plus; Alistair Berg/DigitalVision; Cavan Images/Cavan; Chris Tobin/DigitalVision; Steve Debenport/E+; Hemant Mehta; Schon & Probst/Picture Press/Getty Images Plus; **U2:** Stocktrek Images; Monty Rakusen/Cultura; Rohit Singh/EyeEm; Photography by Thy Bun/Moment Open; Stuart Westmorland/Corbis Documentary/Getty Images Plus; shalamov/iStock/Getty Images Plus; A. Martin UW Photography/Moment; Rob Janné/500px Prime; Westend61; **U3:** Dougal Waters/DigitalVision; Carlina Teteris/Moment; Caiaimage/Lukas Olek; -goldy-/iStock/Getty Images Plus; monkeybusinessimages/iStock/Getty Images Plus; Tomas Rodriguez/Corbis; Tom Kelley Archive/Retrofile RF; **U4:** Maskot; LightFieldStudios/iStock/Getty Images Plus; shapecharge/E+; Caiaimage/Paul Bradbury; Hoxton/Tom Merton; skynesher/E+; portishead1/E+; Hero Images/DigitalVision; **U5:** GSPictures/E+; Westend61; Compassionate Eye Foundation/Dan Kenyon/DigitalVision; Hero Images; Sasha Bell/Moment; Caiaimage/Paul Bradbury; **U6:** Jupiterimages/Stockbyte; oberschneider/RooM; Fancy/Veer/Corbis; Westend61; Hero Images; Hero Images; David Oliver/Taxi/Getty Images Plus; Fresh photos from all over the worls/Moment.

Front cover photography by Hans Neleman/The Image Bank/Getty Images Plus/Getty Images.

Typeset by emc design ltd.

Audio
Audio production by CityVox, New York.

URL
The publisher has used its best endeavors to ensure that the URLs for external websites referred to in this book are correct and active at the time of going to press. However, the publisher has no responsibility for the websites and can make no guarantee that a site will remain live or that the content is or will remain appropriate.

Corpus
Development of this publication has made use of the Cambridge English Corpus (CEC). The CEC is a multi-billion word collection of contemporary spoken and written English. It includes British English, American English, and other varieties. It also includes the Cambridge Learner Corpus, the world's biggest collection of learner writing, developed in collaboration with Cambridge Assessment. Cambridge University Press uses the CEC to provide evidence about language use that helps to produce better language teaching materials. Our Evolve authors study the Corpus to see how English is really used, and to identify typical learner mistakes. This information informs the authors' selection of vocabulary, grammar items and Student's Book Corpus features such as the Accuracy Check, Register Check, and Insider English.

This page is intentionally left blank